PYTHON MACHINE LEARNING

The Complete Beginner's Guide to Deep Learning with Python. Learn How to Use Scikit-Learn and Pandas.

WILLARD D. SANDERS

WILLARD D. SANDERS

© Copyright 2020 - All rights reserved.

The content contained within this book may not be reproduced, duplicated or transmitted without direct written permission from the author or the publisher. Under no circumstances will any blame or legal responsibility be held against the publisher, or author, for any damages, reparation, or monetary loss due to the information contained within this book. Either directly or indirectly.

Legal Notice: This book is copyright protected. This book is only for personal use. You cannot amend, distribute, sell, use, quote or paraphrase any part, or the content within this book, without the consent of the author or publisher.

Disclaimer Notice: Please note the information contained within this document is for educational and entertainment purposes only. All effort has been executed to present accurate, up to date, and reliable, complete information. No warranties of any kind are declared or implied. Readers acknowledge that the author is not engaging in the rendering of legal, financial, medical or professional advice. The content within this book has been derived from various sources. Please consult a licensed professional before attempting any techniques outlined in this book.

By reading this document, the reader agrees that under no circumstances is the author responsible for any losses, direct or indirect, which are incurred as a result of the use of information contained within this document, including, but not limited to, errors, omissions, or inaccuracies.

WILLARD D. SANDERS

TABLE OF CONTENTS

INTRODUCTION 8

CHAPTER 1: WHAT IS MACHINE LEARNING 10

WHAT IS MACHINE LEARNING? 10
HOW DOES MACHINE LEARNING WORK? 13
USES OF MACHINE LEARNING 14
Virtual Personal Assistants *15*
Density Estimation *15*
Classification *15*
Clustering *16*
Dimensionality Reduction *17*
Regression Analysis *17*
Latent Variables *18*
ADVANTAGES AND DISADVANTAGES OF MACHINE LEARNING 19
Some of the advantages of machine learning are: *19*
The disadvantages of machine learning are: *19*

CHAPTER 2: ARTIFICIAL INTELLIGENCE AND DEEP LEARNING .. 20

WHAT IS DEEP LEARNING 20
WHAT IS ARTIFICIAL INTELLIGENCE? 26

CHAPTER 3: SUPERVISED LEARNING VS UNSUPERVISED LEARNING 32

SUPERVISED LEARNING 32
Steps in Creating a Flowchart to Solving a Supervised Learning Problem *33*
Curse of Dimensionality *34*
Semi – Supervised Learning *35*
Active Supervised Learning *36*
Reinforcement Learning *36*
UNSUPERVISED LEARNING 37

CHAPTER 4: HOW TO APPLY MACHINE LEARNING IN THE WORLD 38

HOW CAN I USE MACHINE LEARNING? 38
Collaborative filtering *38*
Doing translations *39*
Name identity recognition *39*
Speech recognition *39*
Autonomous Vehicles *40*
Classification of New Astronomical Structures *40*

Playing Games Like Backgammon *41*
Personal Security *41*
Data Security *42*
Healthcare *42*
Fraud Detection *43*
Marketing Personalization *43*
Search engines *44*
Recommendations *44*
Financial Trading *44*
Natural Language Processing (NLP) *45*
Email Spam and Malware Filtering *45*
Traffic Predictions *46*
DEALING WITH BIG DATA 47
The Big V's *47*
Big Data Applications *50*

CHAPTER 5: PYTHON FOR MACHINE LEARNING **52**
WHY USE PYTHON FOR MACHINE LEARNING 52
GETTING STARTED WITH PYTHON MACHINE LEARNING 54
conda install scikit-learn *55*
Installing TensorFlow *55*
conda create -n tensorenviron *58*
Import tensorflow as tf *60*
PYTHON FILES 60
File Opening *61*
Python File Modes *62*
Specifying the File Encoding Type *62*
Closing a File in Python *63*
Writing to a File in Python *65*
Reading a file in Python *65*
Using the for loop when reading a file in Python *66*
File Methods in Python *69*
Directory in Python *70*
Files and List Directories *71*
Creating a New Directory *72*
File or a Directory Renaming in Python *72*
Removing File or Directory in Python *73*
Errors and Exceptions *73*
Inbuilt Exceptions in Python *74*
UNDERSTANDING THE SYNTAX OF PYTHON 74
The Quotations used in Python Punctuation *75*
Declarations Writing in Python *75*
The Language Structure of Multiline Declarations *75*
The Sentence Structure of Indentation *76*
The Language Structure of Comments *78*
The Language Structure of Python Identifiers *79*

CHAPTER 6: THE MAIN LIBRARIES TO START MACHINE LEARNING AND WHAT THEY ARE FOR 82

NUMPY AND SCIPY 83
MATPLOTLIB 84
SCIKIT-LEARN? 85
TENSOR FLOW 86
PANDAS 89
THE KERAS LIBRARY 90
MATPLOTLIB 91
Basemap *92*
Natgrid *93*
Mplot3d *93*
Excel tools *93*
Cartopy *93*

CONCLUSION 96

WILLARD D. SANDERS

INTRODUCTION

This is a guide that will take you step by step through a wide variety of machine learning concepts and techniques, as well as teach you how to work with complex data. The book is intended for those with an intermediate level of knowledge in working with machine learning algorithms, however, it emphasizes leading you with examples.

Studying machine learning techniques is challenging at times due to some necessity of mathematical as well as programming knowledge, however, this guide aims to demystify this topic and make it easy to understand for everyone. This book places equal focus on teaching theoretical concepts as well as working with real-world applications where you can apply what you learn.

Many people are interested in learning more about machine learning, and in using the Python coding language to help them see the best results. When you are ready to see what machine learning is all about, as well as how you can combine it with your codes and applications to get the best results, then make sure to read through this guidebook to help you get started!

WILLARD D. SANDERS

CHAPTER 1:

WHAT IS MACHINE LEARNING

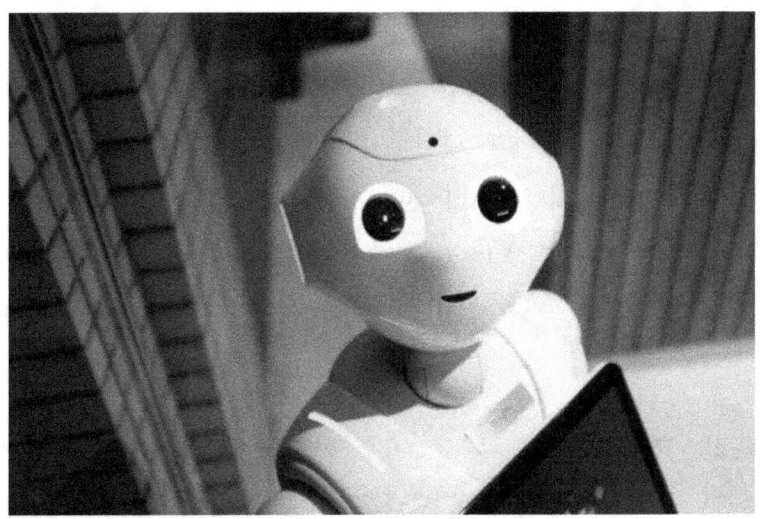

WHAT IS MACHINE LEARNING?

What is machine learning? It is a particular category of algorithms that allow data scientists to create algorithms that can predict an outcome based on the data it receives. Basically, input data is fed to the software, and then through statistical analysis an output is predicted. These predictions can also be made on new data that is similar to the old data that the machine algorithms already experienced. The purpose is to analyze vast amounts of information, perform comparisons, tests, and come up with a solid conclusion without the need for a data scientist to constantly intervene. This naturally requires the creation of sophisticated machine learning models that are capable of accurately predicting results on their own.

If you have spent any time looking up information about technology and where our world is going now in terms of using computers and programming, then you have likely spent at least a little time hearing about machine learning. Whether you were intrigued by this term or only saw it pop up on some of the articles you were reading, you will find that working with machine learning is a crucial thing to know. It can open the doors to new programming that you can do and can make life easier when developing the software and technology that you want.

If you are new to this arena and haven't spent much time with programming, then you may have never even heard about machine learning. Even so, it is likely that at one point or another, you have used machine learning to help make your life easier. For example, if you have ever done a query on a search engine, such as Google, then it was the technology of machine learning that made this possible. Machine learning is the program that runs these search engine sites and helps you find the results that you want.

Machine learning technology is the only way you will be able to get these programs to work. Regular coding is not able to do this complex task. The system needs to read through your request, look through millions of websites, and then pick out the one that matches up to your needs. And in the beginning, it may not do the best job picking out what you want. But thanks to the machine learning technology behind it, these programs can learn your search preferences and predict exactly what you are looking for based on your choice.

This is one of many examples that shows how we can use machine learning to do some amazing things. Not only can the use of search engines benefit from this technology, but you can use it in many other applications, such as trying to figure out whether to consider a message spam or not.

Unlike some of the conventional programming methods that you may have used in the past, machine learning does not just sit still and give out predetermined outputs. While necessary in some cases, it would not be efficient for a lot of the things we want to do. Unlike the conventional programs, machine learning programs are designed to learn and adapt based on the behavior that the user exhibits. This is excellent because it ensures that the user is going to get the results that they want, rather than being frustrated along the way.

If a computer or another form of technology already has some machine learning capabilities or programs on it, then it can be programmed to form the inputs that the user gives to it. This means that the computer can provide the user with the results, or the answers, that are needed, even if the problem is more complicated. The input for this learning process, which is often known as a learning algorithm will be referred as data training in this process.

HOW DOES MACHINE LEARNING WORK?

With that definition of machine learning in place, the next thing that we need to take a look at is how we can get started with this process. Before we look at all the details that come with machine learning, it is important to first look at the way that the human brain is going to work, and then we can compare that to machine learning to get a better outlook on how all of this should work.

For example, most of us know that when we see a plate that has been heated in the microwave, or we see that there is something that we need to take out of the oven, we know that we should not use our bare hands to touch it. But when we think about it, how do we know that we shouldn't touch something hot?

You will find that machine learning is going to work in a similar manner. At the beginning of the program, the computer has no knowledge. To make the machine able to learn, information needs to be passed over Then with this new information, the machines are able to go through patterns using a variety of techniques to help them out. Over some time, the machines will start to identify patterns out of all the data that they have been able to collect in order to make some good decisions

Training data is often going to be given to the machine ahead of time. These will ensure that you are able to get the program to learn in the manner that it should. The algorithms that you put into this are going to help you learn the models along the way.

USES OF MACHINE LEARNING

Machine learning has changed how businesses work and operate in today's world. Through machine learning, large volumes of data can be extracted, which makes it easier for the user to draw predictions from a data set.

There are numerous manual tasks that one cannot complete within a limited time frame if the task includes the analysis of large volumes of data. Machine learning is the solution to such issues. In the modern world, we are overwrought with large volumes of data and information, and there is no way a human being can process all that information. Therefore, there is a need to automate such processes, and machine learning helps with that.

When any analysis or discovery is fully automated, it will become easier to obtain the necessary information from that analysis. This will also help the engineer automate any future processes. The world of business analytics, data science, and big data requires machine learning and deep learning.

Business intelligence and predictive learning are no longer restricted to just large businesses but are accessible to small companies and businesses too.

This allows a small business to utilize the information that it has collected effectively. This section covers some of the applications of machine learning in the real world.

VIRTUAL PERSONAL ASSISTANTS

Some examples of virtual assistants are Allo, Google Now, Siri and Alexa. These tools help users access necessary information through voice commands. All you must do is activate the assistant and you can ask the machine any questions you want.

Your personal assistant will look for the necessary information based on your question, and then provide you with an answer. You can also use this assistant to perform regular tasks like setting reminders or alarms. Machine learning is an important part of this tool since it helps the system gather the necessary information to provide you with an answer.

DENSITY ESTIMATION

Machine learning will help a system use any data that is available on the Internet, and it can use that data to predict or suggest some information to users. For example, if you want to purchase a copy of "A Song of Ice and Fire" from a bookstore, and run it through a machine, you can generate a similar copy of the book using that very machine.

CLASSIFICATION

Classification is mainly a type of pattern recognition, and is usually created through a supervised learning method, where the algorithm is taught using a set of data points and properly identified and categorized learning is already available. Classifiers are algorithms that implement the classification method, but the term "classifier" is also used to refer to a mathematical function that directs and categorizes input data into a certain category, but for the purposes of this guide, classifiers are classification method algorithms. Classifiers are usually created by splitting data points into certain variables, which may have various properties, such as categorical properties of blood types *"A -", "O +", "AB +"), ordinal (tall, regular, short), or even integer – valued (such as for spam filters which count for the number of occurrences of particular words). Some other classifiers are built using comparative observation, which have a function that compares distance or similarity between the two.

CLUSTERING

Much like classification, clustering involves grouping together particular data points or observations based on a list of characteristics that would make them belong in the same category. However, clustering tends to be of a broader scope, and less clear – cut as compared to how classification decides to segment its categories. Clusteringor cluster analysis is mostly used by statisticians and data scientists, especially when it comes to solving problems of information retrieval, data compression, or density estimation functions.

As was briefly explained earlier, the clustering function is usually created through an unsupervised machine learning algorithm, as compared to classification functions that are created through supervised learning. This is because clustering does not emphasize specificity as much and works more to gather similar objects together rather than individually define each object into a specific class.

DIMENSIONALITY REDUCTION

Dimensionality reduction is a type of output that tries to reduce the complexity of objects and simplifies the input by mapping them into a lower – dimensional space, which eventually allows the user to simplify the objects and allow them to undergo feature selection or extraction, which is the process of identifying the most relevant attributes, or "features", in order to be better able to build a model. This is useful especially since there tends to be a problem in the increase of available dimensions and as such, sparser relevant data when objects are placed in high – dimensional space. So, dimensionality reduction is often a necessary factor in making objects more accessible and useable.

REGRESSION ANALYSIS

Regression, a word that many people hear and immediately fear due to its complexity, is a statistical process used to estimate and define relationships between and among various variables. Regression refers to multiple techniques that allow us to model the relationship between a dependent variable and one or multiple independent variables, known as predictors. Regression analysis is very useful for helping us understand how the criterion variable, or the dependent variable as it is commonly known, is affected and changes whenever some independent variable changes, while the other independent variables, if any, remain fixed. Regression analysis is also used to help estimate the conditional expectation of the criterion variable given the predictors, so we know what the criterion variable's value the predictors will be once they are fixed.

However, there are also those that use regression analysis to focus on some location parameters of the dependent variable's distribution in relation to the independent variables.

Notably, due to the characteristics of regression analysis, where the data points fluctuate depending on what is being controlled for, the outputs tend to be in a continuous form rather than in a discrete form, matching the changes in real – time.

LATENT VARIABLES

When you work with latent variables, the machine will try to identify if these variables are related to other data points and variables within the data set.

This is a handy method when you use a data set where it is difficult to identify the relationship between different variables.

There are times when you will be unable to identify why there is a change in a variable.

The engineer can understand the data better if he or she can look at the different latent variables within the data set.

ADVANTAGES AND DISADVANTAGES OF MACHINE LEARNING

SOME OF THE ADVANTAGES OF MACHINE LEARNING ARE:

When businesses perform analyses, they use large volumes of data, and they prefer using real-time data to perform those analyses. It is difficult for human beings to analyze that volume of data. Therefore, machine learning makes it easier to analyze with ease.

Machine learning is improving day by day. Now that most engineers are integrating machine learning with deep learning, they are reducing the cost of data engineering and data preprocessing.

THE DISADVANTAGES OF MACHINE LEARNING ARE:

In any machine learning technique, we always train the model using a training data set and then validate that model using a testing data set. The model is then used on newer data sets to predict the outcome. It becomes difficult for one to identify if there is a bias in the model that has been created, and if there is a bias in the model, the inferences made will be incorrect. Social scientists will start relying only on machine learning to solve problems. Therefore, it is important that some improvements and changes should be made to supervised machine learning algorithms to improve the performance of the model.

CHAPTER 2:

ARTIFICIAL INTELLIGENCE AND DEEP LEARNING

WHAT IS DEEP LEARNING

Deep learning is actually a type of machine learning that is going to be responsible for training our computer on how to perform some of the life tasks that humans do. There are a variety of tasks that could fall into this category, like recognizing speech, identifying what is inside a picture, and making predictions

Instead of organizing the data to run through equations that are already defined, deep learning is going to set up some of the basic parameters that you need for the data, and then will train the computer to learn on its own by being able to see the patterns through many different layers of processing.

Let's dive into this a bit more. Deep learning is important here because it is going to be a foundation of AI, or artificial intelligence, and the current interest that we are seeing in this deep learning is due to how it is related to AI. Deep learning and some of the techniques that come with it have been able to improve the ability of machines to describe, detect, recognize, and classify things in a way that was previously thought to only work for humans.

A good example of this is all of the different things that deep learning is already able to do in our world. many of the algorithms and techniques that work with AIare great at describing the content they look through, detecting objects, and recognizing the speech patterns of those using it, as well as recognizing what is depicted in the images that you present to it. There are many pieces of technology that use this, such as fraud detection, facial recognition, and systems like Cortana and Siri to name a few.

There are already a few developments who are working on advancing what we see with deep learning. Some of these are going to include:

- The improvements that have been done on some of the algorithms have been able to boost up some of the methods that we see with deep learning.

- There are some newer approaches to deep learning that have ensured that the accuracy of the models is going to stay intact.

- There are even some neural networks that have new classes that are developed to fit well for some new applications, including the classification of images and the translation of text.

- There is a ton of information available from companies, much more than there in the past. This helps us to build up new neural networks with a lot of deep layers, including streaming data, physician notes, investigative transcripts, and even some textual data that you could get from social media.

- There are also some computational advances of distributed cloud computing and graphics processing units which can give us all of the computing power that is needed in order to make sure the algorithms for deep learning can actually be done.

At the same time that all of that is going on, the human-to-machine interface that we are used to seeing is changing quite a bit as well.

The keyboard and the mouse that were traditionally used are now being replaced with things like natural language, touch, gesture, and swipe.

This opens up the field to even more AI and deep learning along the way.

This also brings up the question of how deep learning can provide us with a lot of opportunities and applications in the process. A lot of power computationally is going to be needed in order to solve some of the deep learning problems, simply because of the nature of iterations in these algorithms. This results in the complexity going up as the layers increase as well. And you also need to be able to handle a ton of data at the same time in order to get the networks trained and ready to go.

The dynamic nature of the methods of deep learning, and their ability to always adapt and improve to some of the changes in the underlying information pattern, will present us with the information and opportunity that we need to introduce a bit more of the dynamic behavior that is needed into the analytics.

In addition, we can add in a lot more of the personalization that customers want when the analytics comes into play with deep learning. Another great opportunity here is to improve the performance and accuracy of applications, where the neural network is not brand new but has been around for a longer period of time, through better algorithms, and more computing power, resulting in more depth. The next thing that we can focus on is the different ways that you are able to use deep learning to help your business grow and to create great technology that is needed at the same time. To someone who is not all that familiar with how this technology works, it may seem like deep learning is going to be the research phase for computer science and you won't be able to use it that much. However, it is possible to bring in some deep learning in many practical manners to businesses, and it is possible that you are already using quite a few of them today and didn't even notice the technology that is there. Some of the different ways that deep learning is being used today and how we can benefit from it as well will include:

- Speech recognition. Pretty much every industry in our world has seen some sort of use when it comes to speech recognition. If you have ever asked a question to a device, including your phone, to get an answer, then you have used it. Other places like Skype, Xbox, Google Now, and more are using it as well. The deep learning part is brought in because it helps the system to be able to not only recognize when someone is talking to it, but also know what the person is saying or asking as well.

- Natural language processing is another place where deep learning is going to come into play. Neural networks, which are going to be a big component of deep learning, and that we will discuss in more detail later on, have already been used to process and even analyze written texts for a long time. A specialization that comes with text mining, this kind of technique can be used in other places to discover the patterns that are found in places like news reports, the notes that a physician writes out for later, customer complaints, and even more.

- Deep learning can also come into play to help out with recognizing images. One of the more practical applications of this is with automatic image captioning and description of the scenes that are going on. This could be used in a lot of different contexts. One way it is used in law enforcement investigations is to identify some of the criminal activities that are present in the thousands of photos that bystanders in a busy area have submitted. This is just one example though. A self-driving car could also benefit from this kind of technology, so it is able to use its camera from all angles to go in the right direction.

- And the fourth application that we can discuss when it comes to deep learning, although not the last, is going to be the recommendation systems. There are a lot of different companies that are using this, but some common examples of how this would work include Netflix and Amazon. The point of this is to check what you may be the most interested in next, based on the behavior that you have done in the past. Deep learning is going to be used in order to enhance some of the recommendations that happen in environments that are more complex, such as music interests or your preferences of clothing, even when they occur across more than one platform.

There is so much that you can do with deep learning and the world of this kind of programming is bound to keep growing in the future. Understanding what it is all about and how it can work will make a big difference in the amount of success that you are going to see with it over time as well!

It is through the help of this deep learning that your computer is going to learn how to perform the various classification tasks directly from sound, image, and text. Deep learning models can achieve state-of-the-art accuracy, which in some cases, will be able to exceed the performance that you can get at the human level. Large sets of labeled data and neural network architectures are going to be used to train models with some deep learning.

As you can see, there are a lot of different parts that can come with machine learning. It is a great tool that you can use to get your computer or your system to do some of the things that you may struggle with. For example, machine learning can be used to work with search engines and provide you with recommendations when you are shopping online. And if you need to sort through a large amount of data, machine learning can come into play and help for sure.

WHAT IS ARTIFICIAL INTELLIGENCE?

To help you figure out more about what machine learning and what artificial intelligence are, and how they are different, we are going to look at what AI or artificial intelligence is all about. AI is a term that was first talked about in the 1950s, thanks to John McCarthy. AI was first used to describe a method you can use for manufactured devices to learn how to copy the capabilities of humans in mental tasks.

The term is used a bit differently in our modern world, but the basic ideas are still the same. When you try to implement a program that uses AI, you will enable a machine, such as a computer, to operate and think in the same manner as a human brain can. This is something that is going to benefit you because not only will the AI device be able to think like a human; it can do it in a manner that is more efficient than the human brain can do.

When you are first getting started with these ideas, you may think that AI and machine learning are going to be the same thing. But there are key differences. Some people who don't understand these two terms, and how these terms work may think that they are the same. But often, the way they are being used in the world of programming is what makes them so different and unique.

There are a lot of different activities that computers that hold onto artificial intelligence technology are designed for, and these are going to include things like:

- Planning
- Problem solving
- Learning
- Speech recognition

One thing that we can remember when we are working with artificial intelligence is that it is a branch of computer science. In this particular branch, we are going to aim to create machines that are intelligent, and ones that are able to learn and think on their own. In fact, this has become such a prevalent thing in our world that it is known as an essential part of the technology industry, and we are going to see it grow and take off more than ever before.

There has been a lot of research done on artificial intelligence, especially with how much it has risen in popularity over the last few years. This kind of research has been focused and turned into something that is more specialized and highly technical like nothing before. The core problems that come with artificial intelligence are going to be that we need to be able to program a computer for a lot of different traits, and to get it to behave and think in a manner that is almost the same, but faster and more efficient, than we see with a human.

This is going to be complicated, and many programmers, both newer and more advanced, are going to wonder how we are supposed to make this happen at all. And is it really something that we are able to focus on and do, or are we just wasting our time with all of this? You will find that artificial intelligence has really started to take the world by storm, not because it is just a neat theory, but because of all the neat things that it is able to do in the process.

Right now, there are a lot of different ways that artificial intelligence can be used. And some of the things that we are already able to train a computer to do with the help of this technology will include the following:

The ability to move and manipulate any of the objects that you would like.

- Planning
- Problem solving
- Reasoning
- Learning
- Perception
- Knowledge

One of the core parts that you are going to see with some of this research into AI is knowledge. Machines can be trained to act and give off reactions that are like humans, but this is only going to happen if the computer is able to learn off an abundant amount of information that teaches them how the world works. This kind of programming needs to have a lot of information, as well as access to relations, categories, objects, and properties between all the parts so that it can put this to good use and become more knowledgeable.

It is amazing what all of this is able to do if we can work with the technology in the proper manner. When the program or the machine is able to implement some of the artificial intelligence that we are talking about, it will be able to initiate things like common sense, it can start with reasoning and problem solving, and can handle tasks that are really hard to do and kind of tedious, in no time at all.

What does all this mean though? Classification is going to be important here because it is going to help us determine the category where one object is going to belong. And then the regression is going to help us deal with obtaining a set of numerical inputs or outputs to use as examples, which then helps us to discover functions enabling the generation of suitable outputs from the inputs that we are using.

As you can see, there are a lot of different components to talk about when it comes to deep learning and artificial intelligence and learning all of it will take a long time. but understanding some of the basics that we are talking about in this guidebook can help us learn how these technologies are affecting our world, and even how we can use them for our own benefits as well.

CHAPTER 3:

SUPERVISED LEARNING VS UNSUPERVISED LEARNING

SUPERVISED LEARNING

Supervised learning is a method wherein the computer is fed information, usually in the format of a paired input – output data and uses this information to construct a model that will result in improved predictions or in a more favorable output method. It does this by inferring training data through the given "training examples", which then allows the machine learning algorithm to eventually produce an inferred function using the given examples, that will be used to map more examples and will optimally result in determining the classes of unseen instances, which requires the algorithm to be able to generalize results from the training data to unseen examples in a more reasonable way. Note that the paired teaching data is usually referred to as the "vector" for the input half of the pair, and the output portion is referred to as the "supervisory signal".

STEPS IN CREATING A FLOWCHART TO SOLVING A SUPERVISED LEARNING PROBLEM

The first step in creating an algorithm to solve a supervised learning problem is to determine the data type of the training examples to be used. For example, when writing a program in order to conduct handwriting data analysis, the programmer has to decide if they wish to use individual characters, single words, or even entire lines at once in order to train the program. Once the type of data has been determined, the next step is to gather a sufficient sample size of data in order to create the training set to be used for the algorithm. This means that multiple input objects should be gathered, and their expected output counterparts should also be prepared.

Once the training set has been completed, the programmer needs to figure out how exactly they wish their input features to be represented. This means that the input will be converted into a vector, with a number of variables describing it. While it is impossible to perfectly describe the object due to the "curse of dimensionality", the programmer should be able to include a sufficient number of descriptive variables for the computer to have a proper idea of the object. Once this has been completed, the programmer can then determine how they wish their learning function to be structured and how they want to create their algorithm, by using methods such as support vector machines or decision – tree creation, algorithm methods that will be discussed in a later chapter.

Once this has been completed, the programmer can then begin to run the simulation to train their program. Note that certain supervised learning algorithms need a number of control parameters to be determined by the user, and further adjustments may be necessary in order to optimize performance. Once the algorithm has been tested and the program has been trained, the programmer can then try and test their function on a test set different from the training set and check as to whether or not their program is able to come up with the reasonably expected output results.

CURSE OF DIMENSIONALITY

While the "curse of dimensionality" sounds like a very complex concept, and one that comes from a science fiction or fantasy novel, it merely refers to how difficult it is to measure three – dimensional physical objects in the high – dimensional space that data scientists and mathematicians work in, and the various phenomena that arise from this fact. This problem is caused by the fact that as the number of dimensions increases, the volume of the space increases at a rapid pace, so much so that data becomes difficult to gather. One example of how this affects data scientists is the organization of data in high – dimensional space: due to the large amount of data points, many objects look dissimilar though they are similar in reality, which renders many common data organization methods and strategies useless or impractical.

SEMI – SUPERVISED LEARNING

A subset of the supervised learning method, also known as optimal experimental design, it combines elements of supervised learning and unsupervised learning, as unlabeled data entries are included in the training set given to the program. This means that the program learns to calibrate itself through inductive or transudative learning methods, where given the rest of the training set, it infers the proper labels for the unclassified data sets. In fact, the proportion tends to be skewed in favor of unlabeled data sets, with a small portion of the total training set being labeled sets, and the rest being unlabeled data. This can be likened to a math teacher giving worksheets to their students, where the first few problems are already solved, with the solution and answer given, and the rest of the worksheet is left blank. Students learn from the examples and extrapolate the proper method to solve them through the given problems. This method cuts down on costs, as finding or acquiring labeled data is often a resource drain, as it requires a human expert to convert data into a type useable and accessible by a computer. Semi – supervised learning as a method has also been shown to result in higher accuracy in results.

ACTIVE SUPERVISED LEARNING

Active supervised learning is a type of supervised learning where the program is given the ability to actively ask the user questions regarding the label of the data sets. This method uses a combination of labeled and unlabeled data sets, and due to the high cost of manually labeling each data set, the active supervised learning method can be used instead. This allows the computer to attempt to learn using the training set, but if the margin of error in labeling of a particular data set is too high for the program to "tolerate", then the algorithm usually asks the user so that it may properly self – correct. This active participation by a human user is the reason that this method is referred to as the active supervised learning method, and unlike most other methods where little to no human interaction is required once the algorithm starts to run, this method needs a human to be able to fully complete its training set.

REINFORCEMENT LEARNING

Reinforcement learning is a unique method of supervised learning, in that training sets are not provided. Instead, what happens is that the program is left to carry out actions in an environment, and it learns based on a rewards and incentives method, where if their action is correct, then it is reinforced. This allows the program to find different results, and the focus is taken off of correcting sub – optimal results, but rather finding the method that results in the best performance. This method is often carried out by feedback – intensive activities, such as when playing games against a human user or even driving cars. Reinforcement learning is how some programs such as OpenAI have been able to beat human players in video games, and how Google has been able to develop an autonomous, self – driving car. This learning method often uses the Monte Carlo heuristic method, which allows the computer to calculate probabilities in a resource – starved environment.

UNSUPERVISED LEARNING

In unsupervised learning, the algorithm is made to parse through totally unlabeled sets of data in order to train itself. This means that there is a higher possibility for errors as compared to the supervised learning method earlier discussed. Unsupervised learning is generally used more for clustering data and values and sees the most use in statistical analysis where there is a need for density estimation functions. Unsupervised learning is more weighted to finding out probabilities of outcomes, such as the probability of Y for any particular X value, and this is why statisticians are the ones that make the most use of this particular machine learning task. However, when it comes to more conventional requirements such as training a program to recognize or predict particular outcomes given a set conditions, it would most likely be more effective to make use of a supervised learning method rather than the unsupervised counterpart.

CHAPTER 4:

HOW TO APPLY MACHINE LEARNING IN THE WORLD

HOW CAN I USE MACHINE LEARNING?

COLLABORATIVE FILTERING

This is a challenge that a lot of online retailers can run into because they will use it to help them get more profits through sales. Think about when you are on a site like Amazon.com. After you do a few searches, you will then get recommendations for other products that you may want to try out. Amazon uses machine learning to figure out what items you would be interested in, in the hopes of helping you to make another purchase.

DOING TRANSLATIONS

There are many times when we will want to take the words that we have and change them to another language. Whether we are taking our native language and translating over to a different language or taking a different language and translating back to our native language, a good translation tool can make a world of difference.

NAME IDENTITY RECOGNITION

This programming is where the computer will need to be able to look at names and such and figure out their entities. It needs to be able to look at the places, actions, and names, out of any document that it comes across. This can be used in a situation where you have a program that needs to digest and then also comprehend a document that you submit to it.

SPEECH RECOGNITION

Another way you can use machine learning is through speech recognition. This can be a hard one to work with because we have to consider the different sounds that each voice has, how the genders sound to one another, the various dialects that each person can use, speech patterns and fluctuations, and even different languages.

The way someone is going to say a word out loud is going to be completely different than the way someone else may decide to use or say it. And the program needs to be able to catch and learn how to recognize these different patterns.

AUTONOMOUS VEHICLES

Machine learning data also fuels autonomous vehicles or self-driving cars. Machine learning techniques have been used before for training autonomous vehicles to steer appropriately when driving on different types of roads.

Top auto executives are also expecting that by 2025, the world will see smart vehicles on the road through machine learning. These are cars capable of not only integrating into the Internet of Things but at the same time, to learn things about its owners and the environment and automatically adjust to it.

CLASSIFICATION OF NEW ASTRONOMICAL STRUCTURES

NASA also uses machine learning to learn general regularities contained in the data within a variety of huge databases. For instance, the space agency uses decision tree learning algorithms to find out how to classify the celestial objects in the second Palomar Observatory Sky Survey.

Data mining algorithms have been used to deal with problems such as star-galaxy separation. Typical surveys have a sheer number of stars and galaxies and separating them needs to be automated. Mixture modeling, DT, ANN, and SOM are some of the common data mining algorithms used for this problem.

PLAYING GAMES LIKE BACKGAMMON

Machine learning algorithms have also been used in the most successful computer programs used for playing games. For instance, TD-Gammon is the world's top backgammon computer program that learned its strategy through the more than one million practice games it played against itself.

Through these practice games, TD-Gammon is able to play at a competitive level of a human world champion. Computer games using machine learning also serve as learning grounds for other applications such as self-driving systems. Games like The Open Racing Car, for example, help train autonomous cars.

PERSONAL SECURITY

If you have attended a big public event before or flown on an airplane, you have likely experienced waiting in a long security line for screening.

Now more than ever, providing your identity has become essential especially in the digital landscape.

To cater to this demand, machine learning and artificial intelligence are rapidly adjusting to help in identity authentication. Machine learning is proving that it can help in eliminating security false alarms. Furthermore, it helps spot things that human screeners might overlook during security screenings.

DATA SECURITY

Security in the digital landscape is extremely important as malware continues to be a huge and growing problem. Every day, there are thousands of new malware programs created. To combat these attacks, machine learning is being widely used in a broad range of security applications.

Facial Check with Video, which was developed by Onfido, is one of the latest security applications using machine learning. It encourages users to film themselves performing random movements. This can be used for proving the user's identity by checking the user's facial image.

HEALTHCARE

The use of machine learning allows the processing of more data. It can also better detect more patterns than humans. One example of the advantage of machine learning in healthcare involves a study for computer-assisted diagnosis (CAD).

In the study, the computer was able to detect 52% of the cancers in a review of mammogram scans of women, about a year before they were officially diagnosed.

Using machine learning is also ideal for understanding the risk factors for diseases within large populations.

FRAUD DETECTION

Machine learning is becoming more and more adept at spotting the possible cases of fraud in a wide array of fields. It is also proving to have potential in sweeping the cyberspace and making it a more secure place. It shows many exemplary benefits including tracking of monetary frauds online.

One example of the use of machine learning in fraud detection is the way PayPal uses ML to protect itself from money laundering. The company does this by using a variety of tools to distinguish legitimate or illegitimate transactions by comparing millions of transactions that take place.

MARKETING PERSONALIZATION

Companies also use machine learning in marketing. To better serve their customers and sell well, they need to understand them first. When you browse an online store but do not buy the product, soon you will see digital ads for the same product while surfing the web.

By using your web search info, companies can personalize what ads to show you or which email to send to you.

Machine learning and data mining allow them to know you through the websites you go to or links you click.

All this information helps lead consumers to a sale better than before.

SEARCH ENGINES

Online search is probably the most famous application of machine learning. Google and all the other search engines constantly improve their search engine standards using machine learning methods. They use a machine learning algorithm to learn from your responses.

RECOMMENDATIONS

Surely you are familiar with Netflix, Amazon, and similar services, right? These services also use smart machine learning algorithms to better analyze your activities within their platforms. Upon analyzing and learning about them, the ML algorithm compares it with millions of other users.

This helps online platforms like Netflix to determine what other services or products you might like. These recommendations get better every time you use the platform. Any new data about you will be incorporated and learned by the algorithm to refine its recommendations.

FINANCIAL TRADING

Many people out there want to be able to predict what will happen to the stock market anytime and any day for apparent reasons.

One way to predict this is the use of machine learning algorithms, which are getting better and closer at cracking stock market changes.

Today, many trading firms are using machine learning systems to predict and perform trades at high volumes and high speeds. Most of these ML systems depend on probabilities that can turn a trade, with significantly low probability but high enough speed and volume, into huge profits.

NATURAL LANGUAGE PROCESSING (NLP)

Natural language processing or NLP is being used in varying kinds of interesting applications across disciplines. Together with machine learning, it found great use in the interactions industry as a stand-in for customer service agents.

Using machine learning together with natural language, customer service agents can better and more quickly direct customers to their needed information. One example of machine learning and NLP is a chatbot that can translate and interpret human language input.

EMAIL SPAM AND MALWARE FILTERING

Email clients use a wide range of spam filtering methods to segregate email spams. To make sure that these spam filters are updated continuously, the filters are powered by machine learning. Typically, rule-based spam filtering is unable to track the latest spam tricks by spammers.

However, machine learning like C 4.5 Decision Tree Induction and Multi-Layer Perception are two of the ML-powered techniques you can use for spam filtering. Besides spam filtering, ML is also great in detecting malware.

Machine learning-powered system security programs can better understand malware's coding patterns. Hence, these security programs are better able to spot new malware showing 2 to 20% variation in their coding patterns. In conclusion, ML-powered security systems are able to offer better protection against malware and email spam

TRAFFIC PREDICTIONS

We are commonly using GPS navigation services now to locate and get better directions to our destination. When we use GPS, our current location, as well as velocity, is saved at a central server, which is used for managing traffic.

This information is used for constructing a map of the present traffic. Of course, There is an underlying problem – the number of cars equipped with GPS is considerably low. However, using machine learning in traffic and similar scenarios, it becomes easier to evaluate the areas where there's congestion every day.

In addition to the examples mentioned above, machine learning is proving its potential in more ways. Many people use them and experience ML changing their day-to-day life. Now that you know more about machine learning, you can probably see it in different aspects of your life as well.

DEALING WITH BIG DATA

In machine learning, when we refer to big data, we're discussing truly vast amounts of information measured from gigabytes to petabytes. Sometimes the number of zeros that are at the end of a number describing the amount of data just stops making sense to the average person.

The concept isn't new, however. While it was coined at some point during the 90s, the term describes a problem that existed for decades. The concept actually describes quantities of data so huge that traditional forms of data analysis can no longer cope. In other words, when the amount of information pushes the technology of the era to its limits, we can call it big data. There are always points in time when new software had to be coded and new data storing systems had to be built in order to deal with the information appropriately and efficiently.

THE BIG V'S

Nowadays, this concept has evolved to become its very own specialized field within data science and machine learning.

The more modern definition refers to big data as any data that contains a high variety of information coming at an ever-increasing volume and velocity.

This is what sometimes is referred to as the 3 V's in Big Data.

When we talk about volume, we mean the actual amount of data that becomes overwhelming to analyze. Keep in mind that this problem used to exist decades ago, before the arrival of the Internet and the growth of Artificial Intelligence. In a world that is governed by tech, the volume of data can increase only exponentially. Many data scientists have debated on this topic and agreed that roughly every 2 years the volume of data doubles, and the speed doesn't seem to decrease either.

Due to consumer electronics, the velocity at which new data is being created is astonishing. This has led to the development of new ways to deal with data because it either needs to be processed in real time or stored for later processing. Storage space, bandwidth capacity, and computer processing power are all being strained.

Another thing you should keep in mind is that not all data is the same. We aren't dealing with just one format. A large variety of data, whether emails, stock market data, credit card transactions, etc, needs to be stored somewhere, and each storage system needs to be designed specifically for the form of data it needs to hold. This aspect of Big Data creates further complications on top of the storage space problem.

Data is also considered highly valuable under the condition that this value can be extracted. This aspect of Big Data is also heavily influenced by the type of data. If data is not properly structured, it requires a lot of work before it can go into processing. This lower the value of the data, the more unlikely it is to be neatly arranged inside a numeric database.

When looking at recorded Big Data, you should also keep in mind that the quality of it is not equal, usually far from it. The veracity of the data from large datasets has a great impact on how much significance is given to certain information. There are countless reasons why data can be considered or suspected to be inaccurate.

For instance, what if those who collected this data have made assumptions to simply fill in some gaps? What if errors and faulty predictions were introduced in the dataset because of various software bugs? What if the hardware that stored the data suffered from technical abnormalities? Imagine two temperature measurement sensors that record two different values at the exact same time during the same day. Which one is the correct one? When analyzing the data, you can't determine whether one of those temperature sensors was suffering from a glitch or lack of maintenance.

The source of the data can also be suspicious. What if we're looking at a company's data that comes from their social media? There is no way to verify from the gathered data whether that information comes from real users or bots. And let's not forget the impact that human error can have on data. All it takes is one mistake made by a user of an online service when creating his or her account.

As you can see, dealing with Big Data is no easy task. However, the purpose here is to find the valuable bits of information among the noise surrounding it. Governments constantly study such data to improve performance in various sectors. Businesses do the same in order to increase their profits, cut manufacturing costs, and make decisions on creating new brands and products.

BIG DATA APPLICATIONS

Let's take a look at some of the areas where Big Data can be used to make a big difference:

PREDICT DEMAND

Big Data analysis can lead to accurate predictions of a consumer base's demands. We can take in past and present products or services and detect the pattern with the help of machine learning. Finding out the key attributes that made previous products successful can lead us to create new products and services that will have the same potential.

MAINTENANCE

Big Data is used in pretty much all industries, from tool manufacturers to aeronautics. Analyzing vast amounts of data can help data scientists predict when a certain component is going to fail. Information such as manufacturing year, materials, model, and so on can feed algorithms with the right amount of data to make accurate predictions. If such failures are predicted before they happen, maintenance can be called on to solve a problem before it even occurs, therefore significantly reducing the risk of injury or financial loss.

CUSTOMER SERVICE

We all know that one way or another, businesses record customer information or acquire it from companies specializing in data gathering. Keep in mind that we aren't talking here about social security numbers or credit card information. Remember that last time you visited a certain web store, looked at a couple of items, but didn't buy anything? That data is recorded, and it is valuable. You might think it doesn't mean anything to you, but companies can get a good picture of their consumer base by analyzing every little action they take. Social media, phone calls, website visits and more are all bits of data that is gathered with the purpose of gaining an edge over other companies. Analyzing this Big Data can improve the quality of customer service, products, or reduce negative experiences.

CHAPTER 5:

PYTHON FOR MACHINE LEARNING

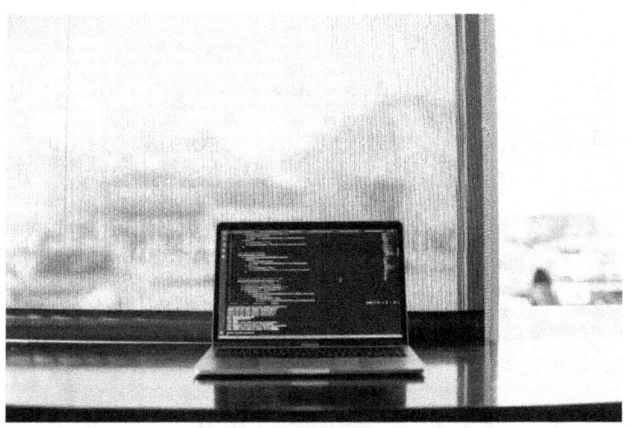

WHY USE PYTHON FOR MACHINE LEARNING

Python has certainly become one of the most popular machine languages in the world because it is quite easy to use and very efficient. The simplicity and readability of Python make it easily understandable. Also, it is considered to be one of the most beginner-friendly languages. The vast number of libraries and packages available certainly make it easy to achieve complex functions with minimum coding.

Applications of machine learning usually work with vast data sets and inbuilt libraries like NumPy SciPy, and TensorFlow. All this makes it easy to develop applications for machine learning and deep learning.

Python can also be extended to work for different programs and that's why data scientists are using it to analyze data. Learning to code in Python is a good idea since it will help you analyze and interpret the data to identify solutions that will work efficiently for you. Python can work across various devices and it is designed using clean and simple syntax- thereby making it intuitive and easy to learn for users.

While we are going to take a closer look at the Python coding language and how it works in a bit, it is essential to note here that we are using Python with machine learning because it is one of the best languages for doing this. Python coding is simple, making it easy enough for a beginner to start with, but it still has plenty of power behind it to ensure that you are going to get the work done. The Python language also comes with a big library, it can work well with other languages if you need to have two or more work together, and it is easy to read, even as a beginner.

There are a lot of other coding languages that can work well with machine learning. But often, they add a layer of complications to the process, and they are often saved for those who know that particular language well or some of the most sophisticated options with machine learning.

The Python language is so much better at helping you to complete your tasks. It is simple to work with, easy to understand, and has all the power you need to work with the algorithms in this guidebook. We will even go through some of the algorithms and show you the different Python codes that you can use to get the most out of each one. There is nothing like the ease of use, power, and variety that you can find when you use the Python coding language, even when it comes to machine learning.

GETTING STARTED WITH PYTHON MACHINE LEARNING

Both the Scikit-Learn and the TensorFlow library are going to need to be set up to start with Python machine learning. But the first one that we are going to work with is the Scikit-Learn. This is a library that you can work with if you have Python 2.7 or higher on your system. If those are installed already, then you are ready to go. It is usually best if you are working with machine learning that has one of these newer versions, so installing that can help.

Before you start with installing this library, double check and see if the SciPy and Numpy libraries are installed already —if these are not present, then you need to install them first, and then go through and install the Scikit-Learn.

The installation of these libraries may seem like it is time-consuming; it is essential and you can do this with the help of pip. This pip is a tool that will come along with Python, so you can use the pip as soon as the system is all installed. From here, you can work with the command below to help you get the Scikit-Learn library ready to go:

From here, the installation will be able to run, and then it will complete once all of that is done. It is also possible for you to go through and use the option of conda to help install this library. The command that you will want to use to make sure that this happens is:

CONDA INSTALL SCIKIT-LEARN

Once you notice that the installation of scikit-learn is complete, it is time to do some importation to get it over to the Python program. This step is necessary to use the algorithms that come with it. The good news is that the command to make this happen is going to be done. You need to go to your command line and type in import sklearn.

If your command can go through without leaving behind an error message, then you know that the installation that you did was successful. After you are done with all of these steps, your scikit-learn library is on the computer, it is compatible with the Python program, and it is going to be ready to use.

INSTALLING TENSORFLOW

Once you have the Scikit-Learn library put in place in your environment, it is time to start installing the TensorFlow library. When you download this one, you can get a few different APIs for other programming languages outside Python, including Java and C++, so if you need to use these, you can get a hold of them pretty easily. You can download TensorFlow on a few different devices if you would like, but for this guidebook, we are going to discuss how you can install this library on a Windows computer. You can use the pip that we had from before, or Anaconda, to get this downloaded on your Windows computer.

The native pip is often the best way to get TensorFlow installed on your system, without having to worry about the virtual environment that comes with it. But one of the things that you are going to need to keep track of here is that when you install this library with a pip, there are times when this will interfere with some of the other installations of Python that are on the computer, and you need to be aware of this ahead of time.

The good thing to know here is that the only thing that you need to have up and running to make this work is a single command. And once you know this command, TensorFlow can install on your system and be up and running. Once you get this library installed using the pip, you are going to see that there are some options, including the ability to choose which directory you would like to store this on.

Now, you can also choose to install the TensorFlow library on your computer with the help of Anaconda. To do this, you first need to go through and create your virtual environment. You may also want to work with a pip for this one as well. Before you start on this one, make sure that you have a Windows system and Python 3.5 or above. Pip 3 program needs to be in place as well to help with this kind of installation.

Pip is a program that is automatically going to get installed when you get Python on your system. But the Anaconda program isn't. This means that if you would like to make sure that TensorFlow is installed with the use of the Anaconda program, you first need to take the time to install this program. To do this, visit the website for Anaconda, download it from the website, and then find the instructions for installation from that same site.

Once you have gone through and installed the Anaconda program, you should notice that it comes with a package that is called conda. This is a good package to take some time to look at and explore because it will work when you want to manage any installation packages or manage virtual environments. To get access to this package, you need to start up the Anaconda program.

After you get to this point, you can head over to the Windows main screen and then click on the Start menu. You can choose All Programs and expand it out until you see the folder for Anaconda. You click on this prompt to launch the folder. If you need to see what details are in this package, you can run a command in the command line for "conda info." This makes it easier to see the details for that package and the manager as well.

There are a lot of cool things that come with the Anaconda program, but one of the main options that you will want to learn more about will help with machine learning. Anaconda can help you create an environment of Python for your own using this package. The virtual environment is going to be its isolated copy of Python, and it will have the right capabilities of maintaining all of the files that it needs, including the directories and paths. This can be helpful because it allows you to do all of these things while still working with the version of Python that you want and any of the other libraries that you want.

These virtual environments may seem like they are complicated, but they are helpful because they will provide you with a way to isolate your projects and can avoid some of the significant problems that can arise along the way. Note that this is going to be a separate environment compared to the normal Python environment that was downloaded before. This is important because you won't be able to have any effect on the regular Python environment, whether it is bad or good.

At this point, we want to do some work to help us create a virtual environment for that TensorFlow package. This can be done when we use the command of "conda create." Since we want to create a brand-new environment that we have called tensorenviron, we would need to use the formula below to help:

CONDA CREATE -N TENSORENVIRON

At this point, the program is going to ask you whether you would like to allow the process of creating the environment to continue, or if you would like to cancel the work. You will want to type in the "y," and then hit the enter key to move on. This will allow the installation to continue successfully to see the results that you want. Once you have been able to go through this whole thing and create an environment, you will need to take a few minutes and let this environment activate it. If you do not do the activation correctly, you won't be able to use this new environment—you won't be able to get the new environment to work, either. You will be able to activate this using the command discussed earlier. From that point, you will then be able to list out the name that you would like for the environment. An excellent example of what we are talking about here and how it will work includes:

ACTIVATE TENSORENVIRON

Now that you have been able to activate the TensorFlow environment, it is time to go ahead and make sure that the package for TensorFlow is going to be installed, too. You can do this by using the command below:

CONDA INSTALL TENSORFLOW

From here, the computer is going to present you with a list of all of the different packages that you can install together, along with the package for TensorFlow if you would like. You will be prompted to decide if you want to install these packages or not. You can then type in the "y," and hit the enter key on the keyboard.

Once you agree to do this, the installation of this package is going to get started right away. However, notice that this particular process for installation is going to take a bit of time, so you need to wait and remain patient. The speed of your connection will determine the amount of time that the installation process is going to take. The progress and how far the installation has gone and yet to go will be shown on a prompt window. After a certain time, the installation process is going to be complete, and you can then determine if the installation process was successful or not. This is pretty easy to do because you need to run the import statement with Python. The statement is going to be done from the regular terminal of Python. If you are doing this with the Anaconda prompt, you can type in "python" and hit the enter key. This is going to make sure that you end up in the terminal for Python, and from there, you can run the import statement below:

IMPORT TENSORFLOW AS TF

If you find that the package wasn't installed properly, you are going to end up with an error message on the screen after you run this code. If you don't see an error message, then you know that the installation of the package was successful.

PYTHON FILES

To understand machine learning you are required to understand how files work in Python. The following section discusses Python files.

Files are used for future storage. To read from a file we need to open it and once we are through with it, we have to close it to free the resources.

FILE OPENING

The inbuilt function open() in Python is used to launch a file.

Example

Start IDLE.

Navigate to the File menu and click New Window.

Type the following:

file_name=open("lesson.txt")

file_name=open("D:/Tutorials/lesson.txt")

Exercise

a. Locate a text file on your computer and open using the Python open()

b. Locate a doc/docx file on your computer and open using Python open()

c. Locate an excel file on your computer and open using Python open()

Additionally, appending 'a', write 'w', or read 'r' the file helps indicate the mode when launching the file. The modes are determined by the context and can be changed as the need arises.

Python also allows us to indicate binary or text mode depending on our programming needs. By default, the file is opened in text read mode. Images and non-text files are handled in the binary mode.

PYTHON FILE MODES

The 'r' is used to launch the file for reading and is the default. The 'w' is preferred when launching writing permissions. For exclusive file creation, we use the 'x' mode. The operation will be unsuccessful if the file we want already exists. The other mode, 'a' is used to launch a file for adding data at the file end while retaining earlier content. For the 't' mode, it will launch the file in default text mode. The 'b' mode is used to launch the file in binary mode. Lastly, the '+' mode is used for launching the file to allow reading and writing.

Exercise

a. Open an existing .txt file on your computer in Python's read mode.

b. Open the same text file in a. in Python's write mode.

c. Open an existing image on your computer in binary mode.

SPECIFYING THE FILE ENCODING TYPE

It is encouraged to specify the file encoding type as it varies from one operating system platform to another and may produce different results if not specified.

Example

Start IDLE.

Navigate to the File menu and click New Window.

Type the following:

file_name = open("my text.txt",mode = 'r',encoding = 'utf-8')

CLOSING A FILE IN PYTHON

The method close() is used.

Example

Start IDLE.

Navigate to the File menu and click New Window.

Type the following:

file_name=open("my text.text", encoding='utf-8')

file_name.close()

Exercise

a. Locate a .txt file on your computer, open it using open() and close it using close()

b. Locate a .doc file on your computer, open it using open() and close it using close().

Important

This approach will exit without closing a file should an exception occur when performing some operation with the file. We will tackle what an exception is but consider it as an unexpected error during execution of a program. The try..finally block is used to cater for the unseen scenarios when attempting to close a file in Python.

Example

Start IDLE.

Navigate to the File menu and click New Window.

Type the following:

Try:

file_name=open("my text.txt",encoding='utf-8')

finally:

file_name.close()

With this second approach, the user is assured that the file will close properly even if an unexpected error occurs interrupting the program flow.

In this case, the close() method does not have to be explicitly invoked as it is done internally.

WRITING TO A FILE IN PYTHON

Three modes are used to write into a Python file and they are the 'w'r for writing, 'a' for appending, or 'x' for exclusive creation. The 'w' will overwrite the file and care should be exercised.

Example

Start IDLE.

Navigate to the File menu and click New Window.

Type the following:

```
file_name=open("my text.txt",'w',encoding = 'utf-8')
    file_name.write("In my first file\n")
    file_name.write("Great file\n\n")
    file_name.write("Has three lines\n")
```

READING A FILE IN PYTHON

In Python, a file must be opened in reading mode to read it. Several methods are available to read a file in Python. If the size parameter is not stipulated, the method will read and return up to the end of the file.

Start IDLE. Navigate to the File menu and click New Window. Type the following:

```
file_name=open("my text.txt",'r'. encoding='utf-8')
file_name.read(5)   # reads the first 5 data
file_name.read(5)   # reads the next 5 data
file_name.read()    # reads till end of file
file_name.read()    # further reading will empty sting
```

Exercise

a. Locate and open a .txt file on your computer using the open() in read mode.

b. In a. read the first three data of the file

c. Read the first five data of the file in a.

d. Read the entire file.

e. Continue reading after reading in d.

USING THE FOR LOOP WHEN READING A FILE IN PYTHON

The for loop allows us to read a file line after line.

Start IDLE.

Navigate to the File menu and click New Window.

Type the following:

```
file_name=open ("my text.txt",'w', encoding = 'utf-8')
file_name.write("In my first file\n")
file_name.write("Great file\n\n")
file_name.write("Has three lines\n")
```

We now include the control statement.

```
for line in file_name:
    print(line, end = '')
```

Note

The file has a newline character '\n'. the print() last parameter helps to avoid the creation of two newlines when outputting.

Readline() for Reading Individual File Lines in Python

Example

Start IDLE.

Navigate to the File menu and click New Window.

Type the following:

file_name.readline()

file_name.readline()

file_name.readline()

file_name.readline()

Readlines() Python Method

For the readlines() method, it will scan the entire file lines.

After reading the entire file, the reading method will report empty status.

The reason for empty status is because there are no more arguments for the method to process.

The read() will go through each line in the file until there are no more lines to scan.

Example

Start IDLE.

Navigate to the File menu and click New Window.

Type the following:

file_name=open("my text.txt'")

file_name.write("In my first file\n")

file_name.write("Great file\n\n")

file_name.write("Has three lines\n")

file_name.readlines()

Exercise

a. Use the readline() method to read each line of a .txt on your computer.

b. Now use the readlines()method to read the entire contents of the .txt in a.

FILE METHODS IN PYTHON

These methods enable the user to manipulate files in an easy and efficient manner.

The methods are preloaded, and the user only needs to understand where they can apply.

Method	Description	Method	Description
detach()	Separate the underlying binary buffer from the TextIOBase and return it.	flush()	Flush the write buffer of the file stream.
read(n)	Read at most n characters from the file. Reads till the end of file if it is negative or None.	fileno()	Return an integer number (file descriptor) of the file.
isatty()	Return True if the file stream is interactive.	readable()	Returns True if the file stream can be read from.
readline(n=-1)	Read and return one line from the file. Reads in at most n bytes if specified.	seek(offset, from=SEEK_SET)	Change the file position to offset bytes, in reference to from (start, current, end).
close()	Close an open file. It has no effect if the file is already closed.	readlines(n=-1)	Read and return a list of lines from the file. Reads in at most n bytes/characters if specified.
writable()	Returns True if the file stream can be written to.	tell()	Returns the current file location.
seekable()	Returns True if the file stream supports random access.	truncate(size=None)	Resize the file stream to size bytes. If size is not specified, resize to the current location.
write(s)	Write string s to the file and return the number of characters written.	writelines(lines)	Write a list of lines to the file.

DIRECTORY IN PYTHON

Python allows us to arrange several files into different directories for easier handling. The collection of files and subdirectories in Python is known as a directory. The os module in Python contains methods for working with directories.

GETTING CURRENT DIRECTORY IN PYTHON

The keyword getcwd() method is used to get the current working directory. The method will return the current working directory in a string form. The getwcwdb()is also used to get a directory.

CHANGING DIRECTORY

The chdir() method helps modify the existing directory. However, the new path we intend to create should be given a string as a method. The path elements can be separated using the backward slash\ or the forward slash/.

Example

Start IDLE.

Navigate to the File menu and click New Window.

Type the following:

os.chdir('C:\\Tutorial')

print(os.getcwd())

Exercise

Use the chdir() to change a directory in the Python root folder on your computer.

FILES AND LIST DIRECTORIES

The listdir() method in Python is used to determine all files and subdirectories within a directory.

The listdir() method accepts a path and gives file lists and subdirectories in that particular path. The listdir() will return from the current working directory if no path is specified.

Example

Start IDLE.

Navigate to the File menu and click New Window.

Type the following:

print(os.getcwd())

C:\Tutorial

os.listdir()

os.listdir('D:\\')

CREATING A NEW DIRECTORY

The mkdir() method can be used to create a new directory. The method accepts the path of the new directory and will create a new directory in the current working directory in case the particular path is not defined.

os.mkdir('week2')

os.listdir()

FILE OR A DIRECTORY RENAMING IN PYTHON

In Python, the rename()method is used to rename a file or a directory.

The old name is given as argument 1 and the new name is given as argument 2.

Example

Start IDLE.

Navigate to the File menu and click New Window.

Type the following:

```
os.listdir()
os.rename('week2','fresh_name')
os.listdir(
os.listdir()
```

Exercise

Create a directory using the Python method and name it Lesson. Rename it using a Python method to Python Lessons.

REMOVING FILE OR DIRECTORY IN PYTHON

The remove() method is used to delete a file in Python. Likewise, rmdir() is used to remove an empty directory.

Example

Start IDLE. Navigate to the File menu and click New Window.

Type the following:

os.listdir()

['mine_direct']

os.rmdir('mine_direct')

ERRORS AND EXCEPTIONS

When the Python interpreter encounters errors, it will raise exceptions. For instance, dividing a number by zero will lead to an exception.

Example of an Error

Start IDLE.

Navigate to the File menu and click New Window.

Type the following:

if y < 3

 if y < 3

Runtime errors can still occur when we open a file that does not exist.

A file may not exist because it has been renamed and we are accessing it using the old name or the file has been deleted.

The file could have the same name but has changed the file extension.

Python will create an exception object whenever these runtime error types occur.

INBUILT EXCEPTIONS IN PYTHON

Python has several inbuilt exceptions that are flagged when associated errors arise.

The local() method can help list all inbuilt exceptions in Python.

UNDERSTANDING THE SYNTAX OF PYTHON

Having examined how Python runs and executes its program, it is critical to examine the syntax of Python in order to give sufficient information to learners. For the most part, syntax implies the rules of the acceptable ways of arranging words for a particular purpose contained in the series of words. In any case, Python syntax describes how the arrangement of words that characterizes how human users and the framework ought to be composed and interpreted as a Python program. Since you have composed and run your program in Python, intimating yourself with its syntax is an absolute necessity.

THE QUOTATIONS USED IN PYTHON PUNCTUATION

In the punctuation of Python, there are bunches of directions done by using the quote. As a matter of fact, Python permits the utilization of quotes to show string literals. Regardless of whether you are using single, twofold, or triple statements, you should begin and end the string with a similar sort to guarantee the program is executed as determined. Note that you'd use the triple statements just when your string keeps running over a few lines.

DECLARATIONS WRITING IN PYTHON

The arrangement of directions given to Python translator to execute and run is called explanation statements. For instance, when you dole out an incentive to a variable, state my variable = "feline", you've recently owned a task expression. Be that as it may, the linguistic structure of a task doesn't live in to that extent or with the citation as task explanation may likewise be as short as c = 3. Different sorts of statements in Python incorporate; if explanations, for statements, while declarations, and some more.

THE LANGUAGE STRUCTURE OF MULTILINE DECLARATIONS

As examined, declarations are known as guidelines. These directions may be more than a few lines; henceforth multiline declaration. While composing code, you'll have to break a long declaration over various lines. To do this, you may wrap the statement inside enclosures, supports, and sections. In view of styles of composing, this procedure is the favored style for taking care of multiline statements. Then again, there is an approach to wrap different lines by using an oblique punctuation line (\) toward the finish of each line to show line continuation. As you compose your own code, ideal comprehension of the multiline grammar turns out to be simple.

THE SENTENCE STRUCTURE OF INDENTATION

For the most part, space is used to indicate squares of code. This is like what is found in other programming dialects like C, C++, and so on as supports. Python is arranged in spaces.

Using Python, squares of codes are arranged by space not by style or inclination but rather as an unbending language prerequisite. Numerous developers have finished up this guideline combined with others which makes Python codes increasingly comprehensible and reasonable. Based on distinguishing proof and structure, a square of code can be effectively recognized when you take a gander at a Python program as they begin a similar separation to one side. If it must be all the more profoundly settled, you can basically indent another square further to one side. For instance, here is a section of a program characterizing the expense of shoes: def cost of shoes ($5):

cost = 5 * $

if 3 >= 15:

cost - = 4

elif days >= 2:

cost - = 10

return cost

It is important to take note of that; you should dependably ensure that the indent space is steady inside a square. When you use IDLE and different IDEs to include your codes, Python naturally gives space on the consequent line when you enter an explanation that requires space. Space, by the principles of Python, is proportionate to 4 spaces to one side; keep at it.

After the formation of space, you might need to realize how to end it. Simply, the end of each space is the end of the square. The third and last syntactic part that Python expels which could be familiar to most learners of other programming C-like languages is that there is no need to compose anything irrelevant in your code to grammatically access the start and end of a bracketed square of code. You don't need to incorporate start/end, at that point/end if, or surround the bracket square, as you do in C-like language like: if (x > y) {

x = 1;

y = 2;

}

In Python, rather, you reliably indent every one of the codes in a given single settled square giving it a similar separation to one side. Note that Python uses the codes' physical space to learn where the square begins and stops: If a > b:

a = 1

b = 2

Space implies, now, the clear whitespace around the two settled declarations. Python couldn't care less to what degree you indent (you may use either spaces or tabs), or how you indent; you have the decision of using any number of spaces or tabs. To state, the space of one settled square can be very surprising from that of another. The general language structure decided is just that the majority of the space explanations must be indented a similar separation to one side. This is in such a case that else you will get a grammar mistake, and your code won't keep running until you fix its space to be predictable. Check everything before experiencing the execution arrange.

THE LANGUAGE STRUCTURE OF COMMENTS

When composing a program, now and then, you'll want to put a few notes just inside your code to give a depiction of what that statement does; such a thing is known as a remark. A remark is most valuable when you need to audit or return to your program for deficiency or change; it is simpler to follow. Also, for different developers who wish to go over your source code, the remark will make it simpler. How you compose and structure remark inside your program is by beginning the line with a hash (#) image. To the Python interpreter, the hash image advises the Python interpreter to disregard the remark when running your code. If your remark is on a multiline, you can use a hash image toward the start of each line. On the other hand, you can likewise wrap multiline remark with triple statements.

THE LANGUAGE STRUCTURE OF PYTHON IDENTIFIERS

Inside the Python program, Python Identifiers are names given to the class, module, function, variable, or different articles. This is any substance you'll be using in Python to compose codes and they ought to be suitably named or given right recognizable proof as they will shape some portion of your program. Here are Python naming shows that you ought to know about: An identifier can be a mix of capitalized letters, lowercase letters, underscores, and digits (0-9). Consequently, coming up next are substantial identifiers: theMovement, my_movement, move_1, and print_what is_world.

Coming up next are exceptional tips on identifiers in Python:

• Within the identifiers, unique characters, for example, %, @, and $ are not allowed.

• Note that 3life isn't legitimate rather life3 is on the grounds that an identifier ought not start with a number.

• Generally, Python is a case-sensitive language. This is commonplace of identifiers and this is the reason the word Happy and glad are two particular identifiers in Python.

- Python keywords can't be used as identifiers.

- When making a class, the Class identifiers must start with a capitalized letter, yet the remainder of the identifiers be lowercase.

- Separation of different words in your identifier is by an underscore.

- You ought to dependably pick identifiers that will sound good to you even after a long hole. This is the reason it is anything but difficult to set your variable to c = 2.

- It is fitting for the future reason that that the more you use a more extended yet progressively important variable name, for example, consider = 2 the easier it becomes at any point of confusion.

Taking everything into account, the syntax of Python has been managed by the 'modules' where you'd need them. This is on the grounds that you will get everything about it independently rather than assembling it. Remember to run the projects as you learn them.

CHAPTER 6:

THE MAIN LIBRARIES TO START MACHINE LEARNING AND WHAT THEY ARE FOR

Now that we know a bit about the basics that come with the Python language, it is important that we spend some time learning the best libraries and extensions that we are able to add into the mix to make sure that Python is going to work the way that we would like for data science. The regular library that comes with Python can do a lot of amazing things, but it is not going to be able to handle all of the graphing, mathematics, and machine learning that we need with data science.

The good news here though is that there are a few other libraries that we are able to work with that utilize Python and can help with machine learning and data science together. All of these are going to help us handle tasks in a slightly different manner so take a look at them and how they are meant to work with Python and data science. The best libraries that can help you to get this work done will include:

NUMPY AND SCIPY

NumPy. This stands for Numerical Python. The most advanced feature of NumPy is an n-dimensional array. This library has a standard linear algebra function, advanced random number capability, and tools for integration with other low-level programming languages.

SciPy. It is the shorthand for Scientific Python. SciPy is designed on NumPy. It is among the most important libraries for different high-level science and engineering modules such as Linear Algebra, Sparse matrices, and Fourier transform.

If you want to do any kind of work with machine learning or data science with Python, you have to make sure that you work with the NumPy and the SciPy library. Both of these are going to be the basis of many of the other libraries that we are going to talk about here, which is why it is likely that when you work with data science, you are going to also add in a bit of library as well.

First, we will look at NumPy, which is going to stand for Numeric and Scientific Computation. This is a useful library because it is going to lay down some of the basic premises that we need for doing any kind of scientific computing with data science in Python. This library can also help us to get a hold of some functions that have been precompiled for us, and it is fast for handling any numerical and mathematical routine process that you would like to do.

Then there is also the Scientific Python library, which we call SciPy, that goes along with NumPy in many cases. This is the kind of library that you want to work with to add in some kind of competitive edge to what you are doing in machine learning. This happens when you work to enhance some of the useful functions for things like regression and minimization to name a few.

MATPLOTLIB

As you are going through data science and Python, there are going to be times when you will want to work with a graph or a chart or some other kind of visual. This is going to make it easier to see the information that is found in the text, in a glance and the matplotlib will be able to make some of these graphs for you in no time.

The matplotlib extension is going to provide us with all of the parts that we need to take the info and turn it into the visualizations that you need for your data.

This library is going to work with pretty much any of the different types of visualizations that you need from a histogram, bar charts, error charts, line graphs, and more.

SCIKIT-LEARN?

David Cournapeau in 2007 as a Google Summer of Code project developed the Scikit-learn. This process is going to be suitable to use whether you need it commercially or academically.

This is designed for machine learning. It was created on matplotlib, NumPy, and SciPy. This specific library has a lot of efficient tools for machine learning and statistical modeling. That includes regression, classification, clustering, and dimensionality community.

This particular library, has been all done by Python, but some of the different formulas and algorithms that you are going to rely on to make this one work will be written with the help of Cython. If you want to make sure that the performance that you get is the best, you will find that the Scikit-Learn library is the one that you need to focus on. It is especially good at building up some of the models that you need with machine learning. And since it is an open-sourced library, and easy to get started with, you will easily be able to open it up and start using it as soon as needed.

Scikit-learn is an open source Python library. This library is often used to implement different visualization, machine learning, preprocessing, and cross-validation algorithms. This is often done using a unified interface. The functions and features in this package can be used for both data mining and data analysis. These functions include support vector machines, clustering, random forests, gradient boosting, classification, regression, and k-means algorithms.

The Scikit-Learn is the library that we are going to take a look at next. This is a great one to go with when it comes to machine learning. This is because the package that comes with this library is going to provide us with a lot of machine learning algorithms and more that we can use to really get data science to work. It is going to include a lot of different parts that can ensure we analyze the information that is fed into the algorithm in a proper manner.

One other benefit that we are going to see when it comes to this kind of library is that it is easy to distribute, which means it works well in commercial and academic settings, and there are not a lot of dependencies that go with it. The interface is concise and consistent, which makes it easier to work with, and you will find that the most common of the machine learning algorithms are already inside, making it easier to create some of the models you need for data science.

TENSOR FLOW

This is a framework that you can get through the Google platform, and it is used when you want to create some models in deep learning. This TensorFlow library is often going to rely on some data flow graphs that work on numerical computations. And it can step in and make the process of machine learning easier than before.

You will find that working with TensorFlow makes the process of getting data, of training the models that you would like to use with machine learning, of making predictions, and even modifying some of the results that you see in the future so much easier. Since all of these are going to be important when it comes to machine learning, you can see why we want to spend some time learning TensorFlow.

TensorFlow is a library that the Brain team from Google developed to use on machine learning, and it is especially effective when you want to do some machine learning on a larger scale. TensorFlow is going to bring together algorithms that work with deep learning and machine learning, and it helps to make them more useful through a common metaphor.

Just like what we saw when we were working on the other library, TensorFlow is going to work together well with Python, and it will ensure that you can have a front-end API that can be used when you would like to build a new application. And when you execute these applications, you will see them done in what is known as high-performance C++.

TensorFlow can be used to help with running deep neural networks, for training, building, handwritten digit classifications, recurrent neural networks, word embedding, and even natural language processing to name a few of the neat things you will be able to do.

Both of these two libraries work well with Python, and they are going to do a remarkable job when it comes to ensuring that you are on the right track with your machine learning. Both of these are going to take on a lot of different tasks, and you will need to pick out the right one based on what you would like to get done on your project.

The next thing that we need to work on here is to set up your environment to start with machine learning and see the results that you want. Now that we know a bit more about how all of this works with machine learning and a bit about the Python coding language, it is time to set up the environment so that you can get started. This is a crucial step to take before you try to start on any machine learning and deep learning techniques. And to help you get all of this setup, you need to make sure that your two libraries—Scikit-Learn and TensorFlow—are all set up and ready to get started. TensorFlow, one of the best Python libraries for data science, is a library that was released by Google Brain. It was written out mostly in the language of C++, but it is going to include some bindings in Python, so the performance is not something that you are going to need to worry about. One of the best features that comes with this library is going to be some of the flexible architecture that is found in the mix, which is going to allow the programmer to deploy it with one or more GPUs or CPUs in a desktop, mobile, or server device, while using the same API the whole time. Not many, if any, of the other libraries that we are using in this chapter, will be able to make this kind of claim. This library is also unique in that it was developed by the Google Brain project, and it is not used by many other programmers. However, you do need to spend a bit more time to learn the API compared to some of the other libraries. In just a few minutes, you will find that it is possible to work with this TensorFlow library in order to implement the design of your network, without having to fight through the API as you do with other options.

PANDAS

The next library in Python that you want to work with to make machine learning and data science do what you would like. Pandas are going to stand for the Python Data Analysis Library, which helps us to do a lot of the work that is needed in the Python world. This is an open-sourced tool that helps us with some of the data structures that are needed to do data analysis. You can use this library to add in the right tools and data structures to make sure your data analysis is complete, and many industries like to work with this one to help out with some different processes like finance, statistics, engineering, and social science. Best applied in structured data operations and manipulations. It is widely used for data preparation and mining. Pandas were introduced recently to Python and have been very useful in enhancing Python's application in the data scientist community. This Pandas library is going to be really adaptable, which makes it really great for getting a ton of work done in less time. It can also help you work with any kind of data that you are able to bring in, no matter what kind of source you are getting that info from, making it a lot easier to work with. This library is going to come with many different features that you can enjoy and some of the best ones are going to include:

- You can use the Pandas library to help reshape the structures of your data.
- You can use the Pandas library to label series, as well as tabular data, to help us see an automatic alignment.

- You can use the Pandas library to help with heterogeneous indexing of the info and it is also useful when it comes to systematic labeling of the data as well.
- You can use this library because it can hold onto the capabilities of identifying and then fixing any of the data that is missing.

This library provides us with the ability to load and then save data from more than one format. You can easily take some of the data structures that come out of Python and NumPy and convert them into the objects that you need to Pandas objects.

THE KERAS LIBRARY

If you are looking for a Python library that can handle data science and data analytics that is also easy for the user to work with, then this is the library for you. It is able to handle a lot of the different processes that come with the other libraries, but it keeps in mind the user, rather than the machine when it comes to designing the interface and the other parts that you use within this coding library. The user experience is easy, the interface is designed to only need a few clicks to get the processes done and it all comes together to make data science and machine learning as easy as possible.

This library is going to work a lot of the modules that are needed for machine learning. You can work with a module that is on its own, or you can combine together a few modules in order to get the results that you would like. There is a lot of flexibility that comes with using this kind of library, and that is one of the many reasons that so many programmers like to use it when completing work with Python data science.

MATPLOTLIB

Matplotlib is basically a Python package that is designed for plotting graphics. It was created because there was little to no integration between the programming language and other tools designed specifically for graphical representations. If you already became familiar with MATLAB, you might notice that the syntax is very similar. That's because this package was heavily influenced by MATLAB and the module we are going to focus on is fully compatible with it. The "matplotlib.pyplot" module will be the core of this basic introduction to visualization. Creating, improving, and enriching your graphical representation is easy with plypot commands, because with this module you can make changes to instantiated figures. Now let's go through some examples and discuss the basic guidelines that will allow you to create your own visualization draft. First, you need to import all the modules and packages by typing the following lines in Python:

- In: import numpy as np

- import matplotlib.pyplot as plt

- import matplotlib as mpl

Now let's start by first drawing a function. This is the most basic visualization, as it requires only a series of x coordinates that are mapped on the y axis. This is known as a *curve representation* because the results are stored in two vectors. Keep in mind that the precision of the visual representation depends on the number of mapping points. The more we have, the higher the precision, so let's take an example with 50 points.

There are going to be a number of toolkits that are available that can help to extend some of the functionality that we are going to see with matplotlib and ensure that we are able to do more with this program in no time at all. Some of these are going to include us going through a separate download, and then others are going to be found with the source code of this library but will have to depend on a few other aspects that are not found in Python or in this library.

Some of the different extensions that we are able to focus on and can really work with when it is time to extend out what matplotlib is able to do will include:

BASEMAP

This is going to be a map plotting toolkit that can be helpful if this is what you would like to work with inside of your project.

It is a good option to use if you would like to work with political boundaries, coastlines, and even some map projections overall.

NATGRID

This is going to be an interface that goes to the natgrid library. This is best when we want to handle something like the irregular gridding of the spaced data that we have.

MPLOT3D

This is going to be helpful when you would like to extend out the 2D functions of matplotlib into something that is more 3D in nature instead.

EXCEL TOOLS

This library is going to provide us with some of the utilities that we need in order to exchange data with Microsoft Excel if we need it.

CARTOPY

This is going to be one of the mapping libraries that we are able to work with that are going to help us with some of the definitions of map projections and some of the arbitrary point, line, polygon, and image transformation capabilities to name a few of the features that we are able to rely on.

There are a lot of different options that we are able to work with along the way in order to handle some of the features of this library. Itt is good for handling most of the features that we would like to see, and most of the graphs that are going to be important when it comes to this kind of data science. For example, you may find that this library works well when we want to handle things like pie charts, line graphs, histograms, bar graphs, area plots, scatter plots, and more.

If you need to create your own chart or graph to go through some of the data that you are handling during this time, then working with the Matplotlib library is going to be one of the best options. It does lack some of the 3D features that you may need, so this is something to consider based on your data. But for some of the basic parts that you would like to add into the mix, and for most of the visuals that you would like to focus on, you will find that the Matplotlib library is going to be able to handle it in no time.

CONCLUSION

Congratulations are in order! You have successfully reached the end of this guide. You have continued with your training and completed the journey of learning intermediate machine learning concepts. You deserve to reward yourself, because data science and machine learning techniques are not easy to grasp, and they can prove to be quite challenging to the uninitiated. Hopefully this book has succeeded in providing you with another stage of knowledge that will allow you to move forward towards the more advanced topics of machine learning. Just keep in mind that you also need to put into practice everything you learn, no matter how difficult it is. Even if you don't fully understand a technique, do more research on your own, experiment with what you know, and more importantly don't give up!

The next step is to get started with some of the coding and all that we have spent time talking about in this guidebook.

There are so many great things that you are able to do when it comes to Python machine learning, and this industry and field is just starting to be explored. Being able to look through some of the different topics that we brought up, and learning how to do some of the work, can make a difference at how well you will be able to utilize this field on your own.

This guidebook explored different aspects of machine learning that you are can do with the help of the Python language. Whether you want to work with supervised learning, unsupervised learning, or even reinforcement learning, you will find that this guidebook has the options that will work for you. We saw how we can break down a lot of different problems and then use the Python coding language to help us get the work done the right way.

The moment you understand programming basics using Python language, it becomes easier to learn machine learning concepts. Machine Learning is essential in everyday life. This book has taken you through many concepts of machine learning. There is no one specific thing that a person can do to learn machine learning overnight. However, if you follow the right steps with dedication and commitment, you will get the results you seek. Combine a number of practical sessions to improve your Python programming skills. If you are working with an experienced Python programmer, follow all the instructions he/she gives you and keep an open communication channel. Get dirty with the IDE and the keyboard.

You might also need to refer to this book at a later date. Keep it and review it as often as you want. Just because you have reached the end of the book does not mean that there is nothing else to learn about Python and Machine Learning. Read more and expand your horizons. It is the only way you will achieve the mastery you seek. Pay attention to Artificial Intelligence particularly because without it, Machine Learning is impossible. Use some of the tips herein to make the world a better place by coming up with your own inventions especially in Artificial Intelligence.

The field of machine learning is growing like crazy. Many computer programmers are interested in learning more about how this works, as well as how they can use it, to see the best results and to help them create new technology into the future.

Keep in mind that in many situations you need to use your own creativity to solve a problem. You need to make the right decisions on which methods to use and what techniques to use in combination with others. Working together with others can ignite that spark and help you find your way towards your goal.

Keep in mind that machine learning is complex, and you need to dedicate a lot of time into researching, analyzing, studying new concepts, and solving problems. This book offers you the tools you need to put the theory into practice and learn how to work with more complex datasets. Keep practicing and never stop learning!

Thank you and all the best!

www.ingramcontent.com/pod-product-compliance
Lightning Source LLC
LaVergne TN
LVHW011731060526
838200LV00051B/3129